WELCOME TO THE ARTS INTEGRATION JOURNEY

This workbook provides an introduction to the insights and questions commonly encountered during campus amplification projects. The goal is to help enable better sensemaking and case-making activities around arts integration, what it means, and how it will unfold on your campus. This workbook is a companion to The Case for Arts Integration book, which is recommended as a reference and source of inspiration. A2RU's Impacts Map, What's Next tool, and other materials can also be useful in this context.

A2RU offers a wide range of resources for faculty, students, institutional officers, and academic leadership including: research insights, workshops, conferences, mini-symposia, decision support tools, retreats, and more.

For more information, contact: a2ru-communications@umich.edu

CREDITS

Research and Authors: Gabriel Harp, Veronica Stanich, Stephanie Gioia
Design/Illustration: Rich Moore, Stephanie Gioia

This project was made possible by the Alliance for the Arts in Research Universities and its university partners, Future Work Design, and ArtsEngine at the University of Michigan and the Andrew W. Mellon Foundation.

The authors gratefully acknowledge the support received from the National Endowment for the Arts for research on impacts.

With thanks to Mark Callahan, JR Campbell, Maryrose Flanigan, Elizabeth Gray, Mary Beth Leigh, Deb Mexicotte, Marvin Parnes, Deb Pickman, and Emily Ryan for their valued input during the design process. Special thanks to Maryrose Flanigan and Deb Mexicotte for iterations and prototyping of the amplification guidebook and workshop experience.

Some context-making activities are adapted from concepts in:

Lee, V.S., Hyman, M.R., & Luginbuhl, G. (2007). *The concept of readiness in the academic department: A case study of undergraduate education reform.* Innovative Higher Education, 32: 3-18.

Additional credits can be found in *The Case for Arts Integration* companion book.

THIS WORKBOOK IS DESIGNED TO HELP YOU:

As a case-making and development tool while working on your own.

To run a workshop in a group (you may want to translate exercises into posters or practice-based tools so you can work more collaboratively).

As a common framework for consulting with a cohort of other universities in an A2RU facilitated experience. Please get in touch with A2RU about opportunities.

Properly applied, the workbook will:

- Save weeks of work
- Provide structure and clarity for your group's work
- Minimize stress for you, your team, participants, and stakeholders
- Accelerate your ability to assemble exemplary case-making materials
- Raise the quality of your messaging

WHAT THIS IS NOT

As much as these questions help scaffold our thinking, this is not facilitation-in-a-box. Working through the workbook won't suddenly create a compelling and persuasive case, teach you how to facilitate a group process, produce quality research, or get your committee or leadership to prioritize or align. To create something of significance, it takes practice to understand the landscape of people's needs, disciplinary traditions, institutional culture and how creative processes can help. Get exposed to work of exceptional quality. Read up on the many literatures to ground yourself in the fundamentals of whatever areas you are working in. Practice. Witness each other's practices. Talk about the individual ideas. Gather evidence over time. Build a cadre of like-minded folks who can add their ideas and stretch yours.

This workbook will give you a good start. To really build something lasting, understand your purpose—why it matters to you, as well as to those around you. Purpose is reflected in the shape of your messages, their timing, and the craft of the materials you create.

BUILD YOUR BASELINE
WHAT IS OUR STARTING POINT?

BUILD YOUR PLAN
WHAT WILL IT TAKE TO IMPLEMENT ARTS INTEGRATION?

BUILD YOUR CASE

HOW WILL WE DEMONSTRATE THE RELEVANCE AND VALUE OF ARTS INTEGRATION TO MAKE IT A PRIORITY?

BUILD YOUR BASELINE
WHAT IS OUR STARTING POINT?

WHAT DO YOU MEAN BY ARTS INTEGRATION?

As you convene conversations on your campus, people may ask "What do you mean by arts integration?"
Use this space to collect ideas about how to define arts integration in a way that makes sense for your campus.

WHAT IS THE LANDSCAPE OF ARTS INTEGRATION ON OUR CAMPUS?

One of the best ways to build the case for arts integration is to highlight bright spots already on your campus.

1. What are examples of activities, areas, projects, groups, and people on your campus?

2. Consult the Case for Arts Integration book for examples that may expand your definition and help you collect the full range of activities on your campus.

3. For each example, identify the departments or units involved.

WHO ARE THE STAKEHOLDERS FOR ARTS INTEGRATION?

List the people, groups, communities, and networks that may care about or have a role to play in arts integration at your institution.

1. Within these groups, list the specific stakeholders (names or roles) to build a complete map of arts integration stakeholders. Who is doing arts integrative work? Reference the departments on the previous page.
2. Who holds a formal mandate for arts integration? Call out those stakeholders on your map.
3. Who else should be involved in the future? Who is missing from the picture today?

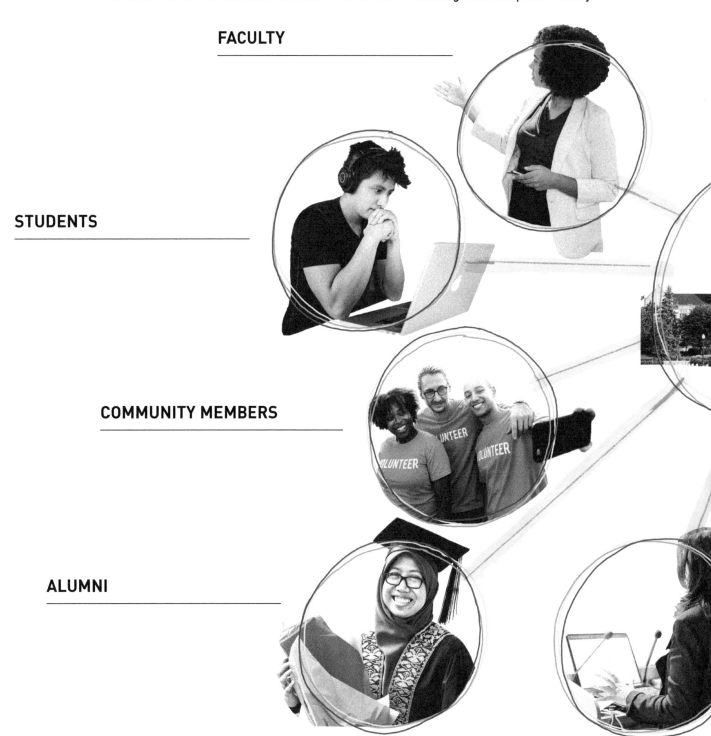

FACULTY

STUDENTS

COMMUNITY MEMBERS

ALUMNI

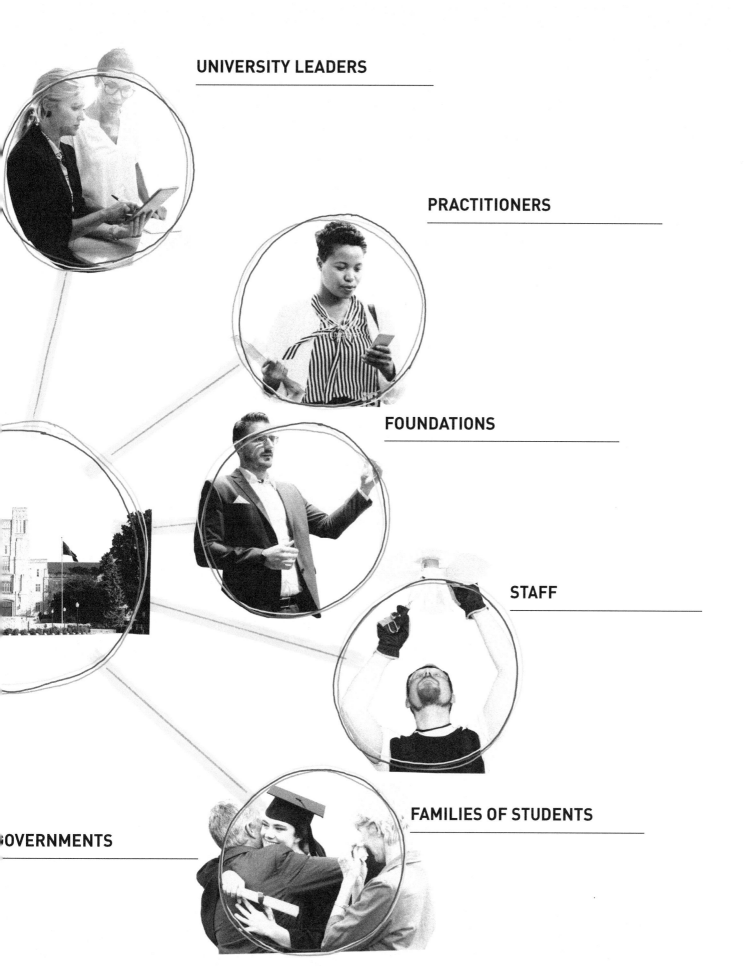

UNIVERSITY LEADERS

PRACTITIONERS

FOUNDATIONS

STAFF

FAMILIES OF STUDENTS

GOVERNMENTS

WHAT IS THE CONTEXT?

The following questions help clarify the context of your arts integration journey.

VISION

Is there a vision for arts integration? How shared or supported is it?
Where is it coming from? Who is driving the effort?

Has any group, department, school, or college developed curricular or research outcomes for its arts integrative programs? What are they?

HISTORY

What has been the history of arts integration here?

Have any educational programs at your institution that integrated the arts and humanities with the social or physical sciences, engineering, and/or medicine been discontinued? If so, why did the program end?

WHAT IS THE CONTEXT?

The following questions help clarify the context of your arts integration journey.

REWARD STRUCTURE

Is there financial support or awards for arts integrative activities? in the department? University?

How seriously is arts integration recognized in tenure and promotion decisions in the department? College? University?

ADVOCATES

Is there a small, cohesive, and protected group already practicing or supportive of arts integration?

Are there practicing and supportive faculty members who teach courses at a key point in the curriculum? Whose research is a model for others?

WHAT IS THE CONTEXT?

The following questions help clarify the context of your arts integration journey.

DEPARTMENT LEADERSHIP

Are department chairs supportive of/knowledgeable about arts integration?

If applicable, are the colleges of which the departments are a part supportive of it?

ASSETS & INFRASTRUCTURE

What assets and infrastructure exist for arts integration? What are the buildings, spaces, and systems that provide support for this work?

What systems are there for courses and curriculum development? Are there faculty specifically assigned to teach arts integrative courses? What is their rank?

How does the university's geography, scheduling, and/or budgeting advance or inhibit arts integration?

BUILD YOUR PLAN
WHAT WILL IT TAKE TO IMPLEMENT ARTS INTEGRATION?

FROM SENSEMAKING TO CULTIVATION
KNOW WHERE YOU ARE...AND WHAT'S NEXT

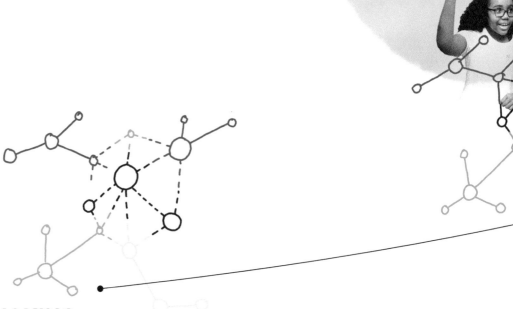

SENSEMAKING
looking for ideas and examples from peers and peer institutions, and advocacy to reinforce early energy.

KEY NEEDS

- drawing inspiration
- looking at examples and case-making
- finding frameworks, definitions, and clarification
- learning from context and history
- mapping and diagnosing institutional strengths and obstacles

Some universities are early in their arts-integration journey, seeking examples and ideas of where that path might take them and advocacy language to gain attention and commitment.

The SENSEMAKING STAGE includes institutions still rooted in a traditional institutional pattern of arts process and practice. Arts and non-arts academic units are mostly independent and siloed. Some cross-disciplinary experiments or isolated initiatives exist, as do boundary-crossing faculty and students, but they are exceptions rather than norms. Arts integration is one of many possible options for next-stage institutional strategy, or is driven primarily by arts units to improve their resources and reach across campus. An interviewee captured this stage, saying: "We're very much in a building and imagining phase – what could it be? If we get the green light, we'll go full speed ahead toward building an ecosystem that permeates the campus community – in curriculum, research, and residential experience."

SENSEMAKING STAGE institutions look to peer institutions for ideas and examples, especially about advocacy to reinforce early energy toward arts integration.

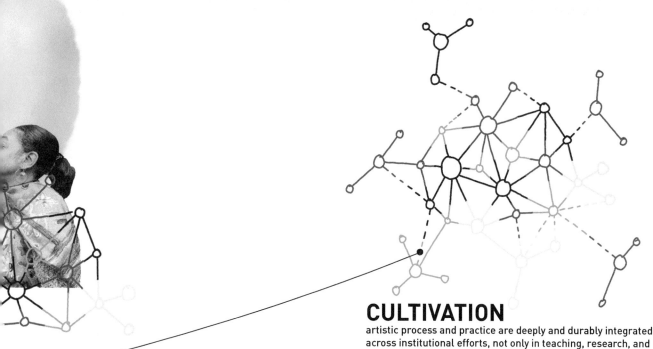

ACTIVATION

having established several ongoing initiatives, these institutions are less focused on basic advocacy for arts integration, and more concerned with operational, policy, and practice issues.

KEY NEEDS

- matching with peers for advice and hands-on help
- operational and policy guidance
- internal visioning, alignment, and coordination; time, space, resources

Some universities are well on their way toward greater integration, but are discovering institutional, structural, and cultural barriers to larger or more sustained outcomes.

The ACTIVATION STAGE includes institutions with on-going and established cross-disciplinary initiatives involving the arts. Through bottom-up efforts or top-down decree (or both), the institution is forging new and evolving connections between academic units and their constituents. Arts integration is a defined strategy for the institution, although often tied to current leadership and n ot yet fully enmeshed in the culture.

Said one interviewee: "I'm more concerned with tenure, structure, budgets, reporting... Some of the faculty models, such as interdisciplinary cluster hires, have had varying degrees of success. Some have been very successful, some not so much. How do we evaluate them? How do we set up fair and equitable support structures? What metrics matter?" Support and connections for ACTIVATION STAGE institutions is assertively peer-to-peer; one interviewee commented, "When I went to last fall's conference, it was very clear to me that it was a place for universities to showcase unique collaborations, methods of arts integration, and we belonged there. We found great examples of how administrative offices can support work that is truly unique – outside the bubble of discipline or department." Still another interviewee found that locating peer institutions can take some time: "When my deans came to a2ru conferences, they found a lot of debate about how to arts might become more vital in the institution. We have multiple arts schools already. Our place, energy, visibility, entanglement is already set. It's not a question for us."

CULTIVATION

artistic process and practice are deeply and durably integrated across institutional efforts, not only in teaching, research, and service, but also in institutional planning, strategy, incentive systems, and infrastructure. Current academic and institutional leadership promote these ideals, and they also seek out these values in any search for new leadership.

KEY NEEDS

- strategy, incentive systems, infrastructure, leadership, partnerships, evaluation, foresight, and sharing
- peer-to-peer expertise and review
- benchmarking, evaluation, and reporting
- research insights and deep experience

Some universities have already integrated the arts deeply across campus in durable ways, but face systemic issues within and beyond their institutions.

The CULTIVATION STAGE might be considered aspirational rather than actualized just yet. In these institutions, artistic process and practice are deeply and durably integrated across institutional efforts, not only in teaching, research, and service, but also in institutional planning, strategy, incentive systems, and infrastructure. They don't only have current academic and institutional leadership that promote these ideals, they also seek out these values in any search for new leadership. One arts-dean interviewee suggested they were approaching this stage by saying, "We're everyone's favorite dance partner. Sustainability, business, education, nursing. All of them see us as a key partner in their research, joint degrees, and community work."

Concerns at this CULTIVATION STAGE stage are beyond advocacy, beyond bridge-building, and perhaps beyond even the language of "arts integration" since the larger focus is on integral work – where all ways of knowing have an important role and an equal voice. At this stage, institutions need an entire ecosystem of like-minded partners to encourage and evaluate new types of faculty, new forms of research, and cross-disciplinary students. For example, they may have robust tenure and promotion guidelines, inclusive of arts process and practice, but they may struggle to find external reviewers with the expertise and insight to evaluate faculty actions. Their presidents and provosts may feel entirely detached from their immediate peer group, and eager for peers who understand their worldview and work-view.

COMMON OBSTACLES

Common obstacles you might recognize include:

DIFFERENT WORLDS

Integrating the arts with other fields implies the coming together of different worlds. Structurally, differences between college- and school-level systems lead to logistic roadblocks. Personally, collaborators face stereotypes, lack of shared content understanding, differing practices and epistemologies, and communication difficulties.

LACK OF RECOGNITION FOR THE ARTS

Interdisciplinary initiatives often don't include concrete investment in arts integration. In many instances, there is a perceived inequity, that the arts are lesser than other disciplines.

TOP-LEVEL LACK OF SUPPORT

University systems that dis-incentivize interdisciplinary collaboration (for example, through Tenure and Promotion policies), an atmosphere that is inhospitable to the arts, and a lack of leadership committed to positive change can all undermine bottom-up efforts at arts integration.

SCARCITY

When institutional systems are not set up for integration, there can be a lack of time, money, space, and human resources.

What are some barriers to implementation that you've seen? How were they overcome? Or, what is needed to overcome them?

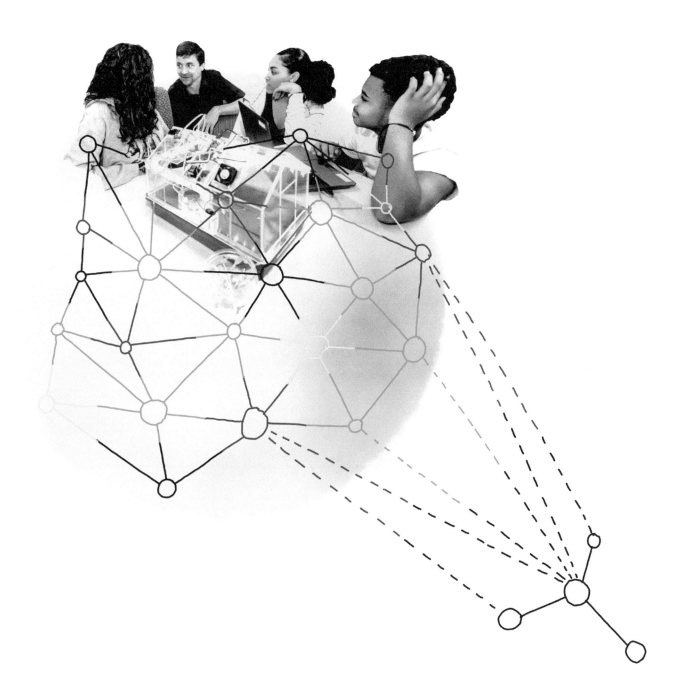

COMPETING VALUES

1. Mark on the continuums below where your organization's dominant culture and values tend to fall.

2. Is there a set of values shared by your arts integration team or another group that runs counter to the organization's dominant culture or the values of another department? Mark the values of your arts integration team in a different color.

STABILITY
Focused on routines and customs, stability, obedience, cooperation, and adherence to expected norms.

AUTONOMY
Cultivating flexibility, divergence, exploration, deviance, and diversity.

PRACTICAL
Emphasizing pragmatism, small wins, immediate gains, thrift, a hands-on approach.

VISIONARY
Engaging in big, paradigm-shifting challenges, problems, ideas, futures, activities, methods, and technologies.

ACHIEVEMENT
Motivated by measured achievement, action, opportunity, risk-taking, and success.

RELATIONSHIPS
Motivated by collegiality, cohesion, social networks, relationships, sacrifice, concern, and maintaining quality of life.

AMBIGUITY
Willing to undertake sustained engagement even if the outcome is not known ahead of time. Language and terms are open to interpretation and improvisation.

CLARITY
Undertakes sustained engagement by resolving ambiguity and uncertainties. The meaning of words and terms is literal and specific.

TOP-DOWN
High institutional priority, driven by leadership through multiple units with resources and specific goals.

BOTTOM-UP
Driven by staff, faculty, or students—without much in the way of formal support—and could be characterized as a "labor of love."

WHAT DO YOU WANT TO DO?

Circle your priorities. Add any that are missing.

I'm looking for ideas and examples.

I'm just getting started.

I'd like to become aware of common pitfalls and quagmires.

I'm trying to find my peers.

I'm trying to build alliances.

I'm trying to make a case for support to my stakeholders.

I'm finding and sharing our strengths.

I'm looking for frameworks and tools.

I'm looking to build internal alignment.

I am making the case for a grant.

I want to know more about what others are doing.

I want examples of projects and programs.

I need help with measurement and assessment of my current or future project/program.

I want to initiate and facilitate cross-campus initiatives.

I'm trying to change the culture at my university.

I'm figuring out how to get things institutionalized.

I'm trying to design new pedagogy.

My goal is to create interdisciplinary experiences for students.

We're trying to anticipate social change to reorient the institution.

I'm looking for evidence of cross-unit connections within our institution.

We're trying to build acceptance for different cultures of evidence and modes of scholarship.

I'm on a committee to revamp our RTP policy so that it aligns with arts-integrative values.

I need to find funding for our big ideas.

I'm looking for examples of other successful institutes and centers.

We have funding for a new student-centered space, and we're seeking proposals.

My faculty need appropriate external reviewers for their tenure portfolios.

If you have more than 3 goals, consider further prioritization. Map each potential goal into this framework.

Pare down your list, focusing on only a few high impact/high effort goals, plus your high impact/low effort goals. Deprioritize lower impact goals.

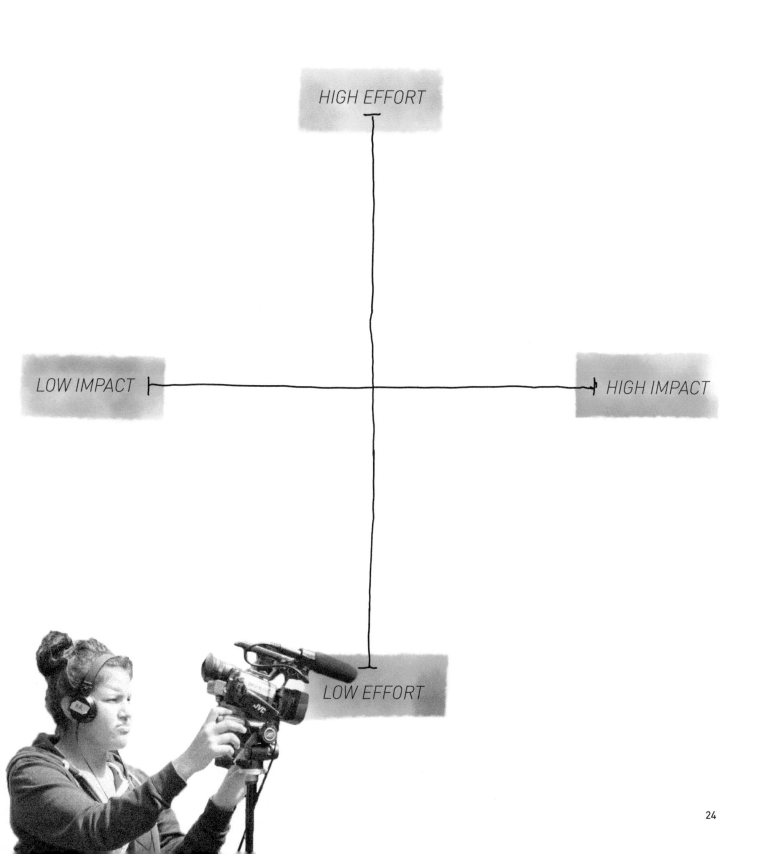

HIGH EFFORT

LOW IMPACT

HIGH IMPACT

LOW EFFORT

NEXT STEPS

BUILD YOUR CASE

HOW WILL WE DEMONSTRATE THE RELEVANCE AND VALUE OF ARTS INTEGRATION TO MAKE IT A PRIORITY?

PULL YOUR STORY TOGETHER.

A strong case typically includes all the components we have built in this workbook. There are many ways to tell your story, depending on the audience. By completing this canvas you have a one page reference of the most important points you'll want to make.

THE CASE FOR ARTS INTEGRATION

What are we doing today? (page 5-6, 12, 14) ⟶

Who benefits? (page 7-8)

TOMORROW

Trends (page 35-36)

Vision (page 4, 9, 39-40)

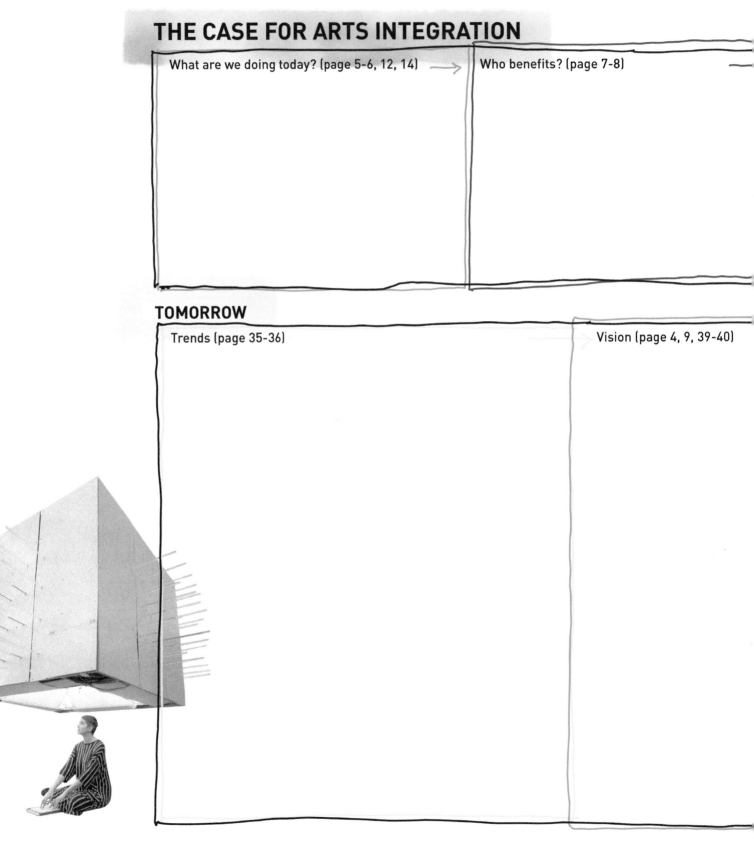

UNIVERSITY: _____   AUDIENCE: _____

Impacts (page 31)   Evidence (page 32)

Outcomes (page 41)

MAKE THE CASE FOR IMPACT ACHIEVED SO FAR

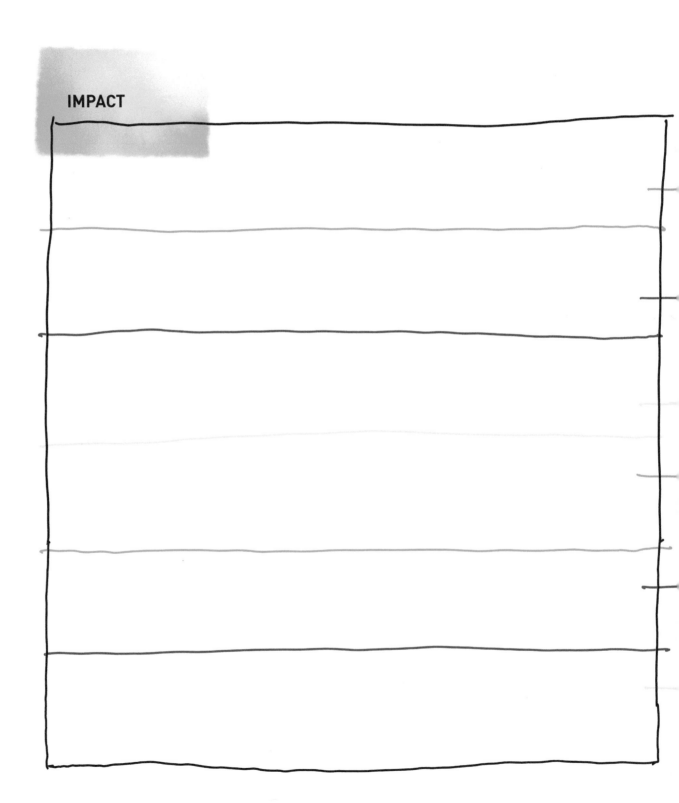

IMPACT

1. Identify impacts. Use the impact map on the next page to circle those impacts that arts integration has had on your campus to date. Add any that are missing.

2. Narrow your case. On which groups or areas is the impact of your work the greatest? Which of the impacts you claim are strongest? Write the top 6 most persuasive impacts below.

3. Gather evidence. How do you know your work has the impact you claim?

   a. What evidence do you have? Brainstorm the ways in which you have seen impact (e.g., quality of student work, attitude of colleagues, community reaction, attendance numbers, mention in the press, perceived change in priorities of your discipline).

   b. Among your stakeholders, what types of evidence tends to be most accepted, compelling, memorable, repeated, and referenced? Put a star next to the evidence that is most "valuable" in these ways.

   c. Make notes on how you could present your evidence (e.g., pictures, video, storytelling, charts or graphs, Impacts Map).

EVIDENCE

THE CASE FOR ARTS INTEGRATION

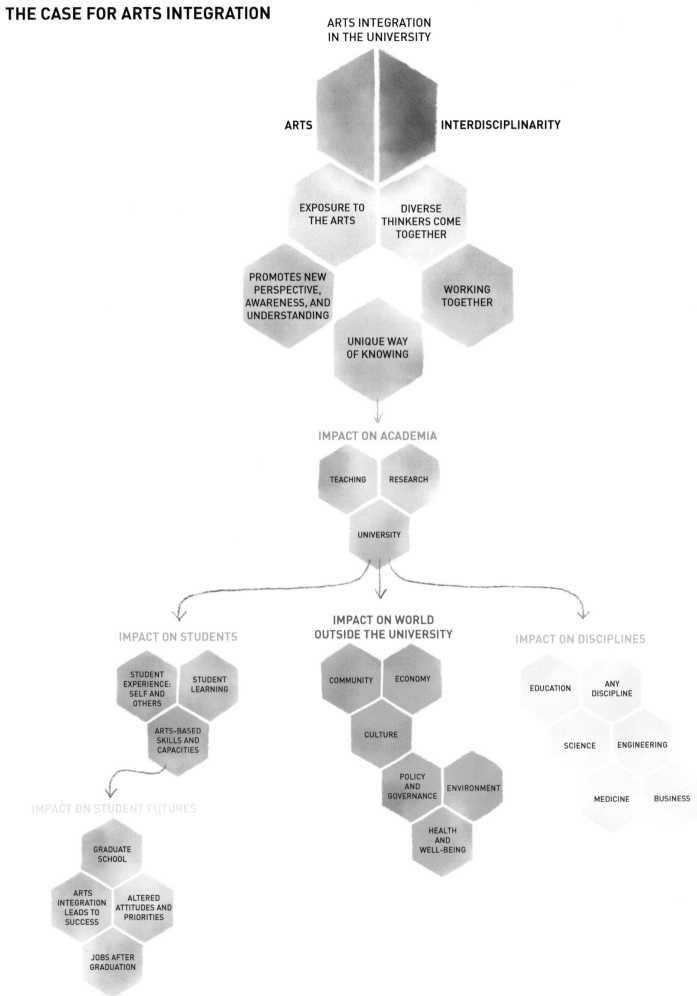

ARTS INTEGRATION
IN THE UNIVERSITY

ARTS

INTERDISCIPLINARITY

EXPOSURE TO
THE ARTS

DIVERSE
THINKERS COME
TOGETHER

PROMOTES NEW
PERSPECTIVE,
AWARENESS, AND
UNDERSTANDING

WORKING
TOGETHER

UNIQUE WAY
OF KNOWING

IMPACT ON ACADEMIA

TEACHING

RESEARCH

UNIVERSITY

IMPACT ON STUDENTS

STUDENT
EXPERIENCE:
SELF AND
OTHERS

STUDENT
LEARNING

ARTS-BASED
SKILLS AND
CAPACITIES

IMPACT ON STUDENT FUTURES

GRADUATE
SCHOOL

ARTS
INTEGRATION
LEADS TO
SUCCESS

ALTERED
ATTITUDES AND
PRIORITIES

JOBS AFTER
GRADUATION

IMPACT ON WORLD
OUTSIDE THE UNIVERSITY

COMMUNITY

ECONOMY

CULTURE

POLICY
AND
GOVERNANCE

ENVIRONMENT

HEALTH
AND
WELL-BEING

IMPACT ON DISCIPLINES

EDUCATION

ANY
DISCIPLINE

SCIENCE

ENGINEERING

MEDICINE

BUSINESS

Promotes new perspective, awareness, and understanding

engagement with the arts

appreciation for the arts

broader perspective

open mind

beyond disciplinary boundaries

new understanding

new experience

thinking differently

refreshed thinking

appreciation for the physical world

connections to other people and other resources

promotes cross-cultural awareness and tolerance

challenge habits and certitude

frame familiar problems in new ways

Working together

diverse thinkers work together

create academic community

stronger teams

better outcomes

lays foundation for future collaboration

fun

Teaching

Co-teachers affect each other's teaching

Faculty bring elements of their research into the classroom

Change in classroom culture

Reach different types of learners in different ways

Increased use of active learning strategies

Promote complexity in learning experience

Provide opportunity for synthesis and personal meaning-making

Research

New research methodologies

Classroom becomes a catalyst for research

Co-teachers affect each other's research

Co-teachers develop research partnerships

University

Strengthen connection between university and surrounding community

Class as opportunity to engage with other disciplines

Provide a space for engagement

Curricular change

Impact on Students
Student experience: self and others

Holistic Growth and Development

Transformation"

Improved social bonds and skills

Increased Civic Engagement

Stronger Sense of Self, Identity

Intrinsic Impacts of the Arts

Positive Experience

Finding Balance in Life

Purpose and Meaning

Student learning

Increased risk-taking

Show knowledge in multiple ways

Improved attitude/increased motivation to learn

Make connections between domains and ideas

Improved long-term retention of content

Various positive cognitive effects

Provide practical experience

Arts-based skills and capacities

Creativity

Personal Expression

Resilience

Patience

Abstract thinking

Envisioning and imagining

Critical thinking

Spatial reasoning

Communication skills

Leadership skills

Problem-solving

Self-confidence

Stretch, explore, take risks

Empathy

Tolerance for ambiguity

Reflection, Contemplation

Organization and Time Management)

Responsibility

Work ethic, discipline

Persistence, sustained engagement

Respect

Observation, attention to detail

Technical arts skills

Impact on student futures

Graduate school

Arts integration leads to success

Altered attitudes and priorities

Jobs after graduation

Impact on Disciplines
Any discipline

New perspective

Diverse thinkers come together

Education

Students become better teachers

Education-focused projects yield positive outcomes

Research products for the classroom

Increased support for arts-integrated teaching

Science

Creation of new technology

Scientific insight

Opportunity for scientific study

Increased connection to public/community of impact

Medicine

Reduce stress and burnout for medical professionals

Improved observation skills for diagnosis

Empathy, tolerance for ambiguity

Engineering

Creativity, tolerance for ambiguity

Business

Creativity, tolerance for ambiguity

Impact Outside the University
Community

Create something new that fulfills a need

Improve community image and status

Build community identity and pride

Build social capital – getting people involved and organized

Economic development – income, visitors, multiplier effects

Culture

Arts as integral to culture

Arts affecting a particular culture

Create products that are themselves cultural artifacts

Economy

Economic development

Profitable business grows out of research

Policy and governance

Environment

Environmentally focused research

University/industry partnerships for environmentally friendly work

Arts-based projects engage a broader population in environmental issues

Health and well-being

Promote well-being

Communicate medical information

FIND CONNECTIONS WITH EXTERNAL TRENDS

Strengthen the case for arts integration by connecting it to external trends. Use the chart here call out which of the trends outlined in The Case for Arts Integration book are in play at your institution. There is also space to capture other trends impacting your university, from changing student needs to funding shifts.

PERSONALIZED LEARNING PATHWAYS

PUBLICLY ENGAGED KNOWLEDGES

DISRUPTION & MIGRATION

POP-UP COMMUNITIES

DIVERSITY, EQUITY, INCLUSION

REGIONAL CONTEXT

INDUSTRY/EMPLOYER NEEDS

STUDENT NEEDS

DISCIPLINE-DRIVEN INTERESTS

FUNDING CHANGES

OTHER

What trends in this area affect our university?	How might arts integration be part of a response to this trend?

IDENTIFY RELEVANT PEER PROGRAMS THAT MODEL YOUR ASPIRATION

Who are our peer institutions? In what ways are we being compared?

Use the Case for Arts Integration book to identify success stories that can be used to build your case. Look beyond the book to capture other examples that can be put forward to capture your insitution's aspiration.

ARTICULATE A VISION FOR ARTS INTEGRATION ON YOUR CAMPUS.

What is the vision for arts integration?

TODAY

FUTURE

CLAIM THE OUTCOMES YOU HOPE TO CREATE

What should be different as a result? What measurable results might you see in the future?

FIND CONNECTIONS WITH YOUR UNIVERSITY GOALS

Our university mission statement:

Which archetype(s) below does your mission statement most sound like?	Ideas for connecting your mission to arts integration
"Empowering students with a transformative educational experiences that prepare them for success."	Arts-integrated classrooms give students a range of conceptual and hands-on experiences, as well as skills and capacities that help them succeed in a range of endeavors post-graduation.
"Supporting faculty development with academic community and a robust exchange of ideas."	Promoting collaboration between the arts/design and other parts of campus enables faculty—as co-teachers and as research partners—to engage with concepts, practices, and people that can refresh and inspire.
"Discovering, preserving, critically examining, transmitting, and advancing knowledge."	Integrating the arts with, for example, STEM fields engenders excellence in teaching, research, scholarship, and creative endeavors—avenues that intersect and ultimately lead to a range of knowledges.
"Modelling a diverse, welcoming, inclusive, and democratic society."	Inherent in arts integration initiatives is a coming together of diverse ways of knowing and working; their success depends on the mutual respect among interdisciplinary players. As such, it becomes a microcosm of the university.
"Promoting the cultural, economic, and intellectual condition of those beyond the campus walls."	Whether a university focuses this aspect of its mission on its alumni, state, nation, or the world, the arts can play a key role in this outward-facing, service-oriented goal. From publicly-engaged artworks to arts-integrated research that results in life-changing medical discovery or engineering innovation, the impacts of arts integration in the university resonate well beyond the campus.
"Setting the standard as a national and international leader."	Successfully implementing arts integration programming positions universities to lead, anticipating—rather than merely reacting to—future challenges.

NOTES